AIRCRAFT

Written by
Ian Graham

Barnes &Noble
BOOKS
NEW YORK

ACKNOWLEDGMENTS

Illustrated by
Julian Baker, Bob Corley, Dave Fisher, Mick Gillah,
David Graham, Stuart Lafford, Steve Seymour, Tony
Smith, Clive Spong, Roger Stewart, Brian Watson

Picture credits
12 Imperial War Museum
25 Imperial War Museum
34 Lockheed Advanced Development Company

*The Publishers would also like to thank the following
for their assistance*
Air France, France
Boeing International, USA
Books International, England
British Airways, England
Bundesarchiv, Germany
Canadair, Canada
Imperial War Museum, England
Lockheed Advanced Development Company, USA
RAF Museum, England
Rolls-Royce, England

This edition published by Barnes & Noble Inc., by
arrangement with Andromeda Oxford Limited

1995 Barnes & Noble Books
Planned and produced by
Andromeda Oxford Limited
11-15 The Vineyard
Abingdon
Oxon OX14 3PX

Copyright © Andromeda Oxford Limited 1995

Reprinted 1997

ISBN 1-56619-870-4

Printed in Italy by Graphicom

Contents

What is an aircraft?

An aircraft is a flying machine. Gliders, fighters, bombers, helicopters, airships and airliners are all types of aircraft. Indeed, so varied are today's aircraft and the tasks to which they are put, that it is difficult to believe that modern aviation really only began little more than 90 years ago. The fascination with flying has inspired mankind for thousands of years, and as long ago as the fifteenth century the inventor Leonardo da Vinci had designed flying machines – but it is doubtful whether they were ever built and tested.

Our story, however, begins at the start of the twentieth century when two American brothers, Wilbur and Orville Wright, made the first successful powered aircraft flight. From this achievement have come all of today's complex flying machines. In this book we look at a variety of the world's great aircraft – each one chosen because it represents a landmark in the development of flight. Because many of these aircraft were later modified, we often show more than one version to illustrate the variety of designs which were created.

FLYING THE FLAG
Many civilian and military aircraft carry badges and insignia. These are often based on a country's national colors, and are equivalent to the flags flown on ships.

CIVILIAN AIRCRAFT
Civilian aircraft are designed to carry passengers or cargo. The passenger cabins of large airliners are pressurized so that the passengers can breathe normally in the thin air high above the ground.

HELICOPTERS
Instead of wings, helicopters have long, thin rotor blades that whirl around. The spinning rotor blades enable helicopters to take off and land vertically, so they do not need the long runways that airplanes with wings require.

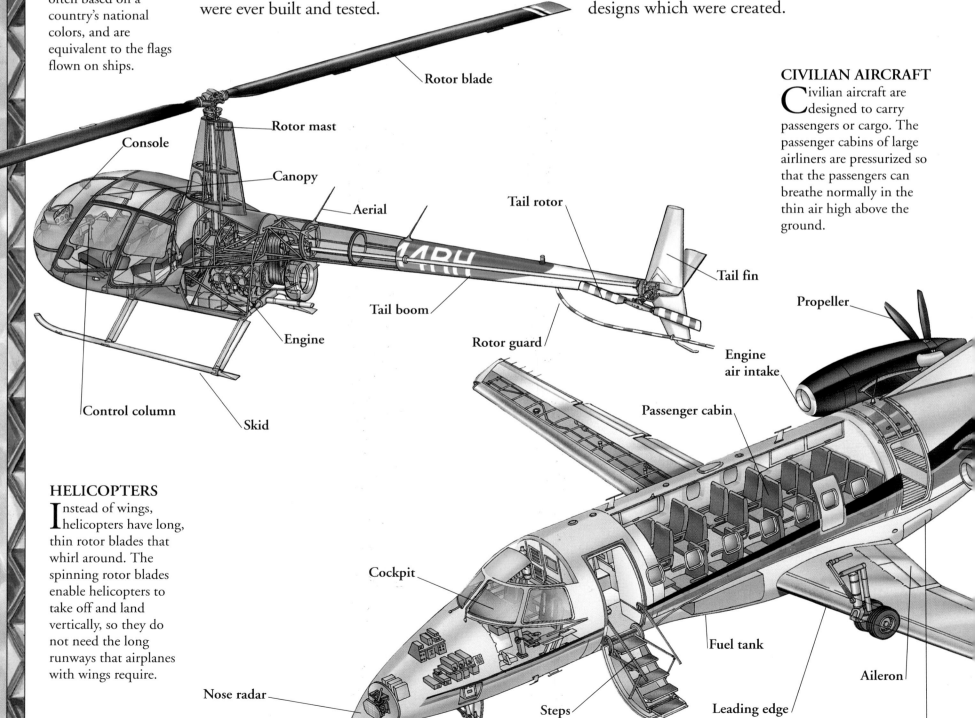

Rotor blade

Rotor mast

Console

Canopy

Aerial

Tail rotor

Tail fin

Tail boom

Rotor guard

Engine

Control column

Skid

Propeller

Engine air intake

Passenger cabin

Cockpit

Fuel tank

Aileron

Nose radar

Steps

Leading edge of wing

Cargo bay door

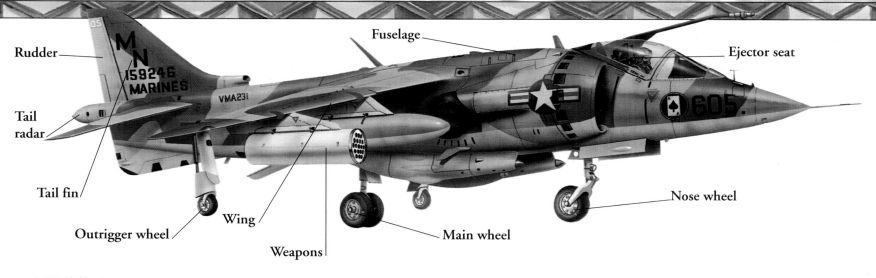

Rudder

Tail radar

Tail fin

Outrigger wheel

Wing

Weapons

Fuselage

Ejector seat

Nose wheel

Main wheel

MILITARY AIRCRAFT

Military aircraft perform a variety of different roles for armies, air forces and navies. Fighters attack other aircraft. Bombers drop bombs or fire missiles. Transport aircraft carry troops and vehicles. Reconnaissance aircraft spy on the enemy.

Elevator

Static dischargers

Exhaust nozzle

Engine

Trailing edge of wing

Navigation light

PRINCIPLES OF FLIGHT

All heavier-than-air aircraft have wings or rotor blades to lift them into the air, and all except gliders have engines to thrust them forward fast enough to gain lift. Craft such as airships create lift in a different way, using lighter-than-air gas.

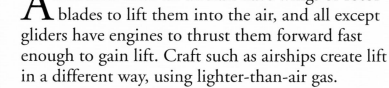

Lift

Thrust

Drag

Weight

LIFT, DRAG, THRUST, WEIGHT

Every airplane has four forces acting on it. Its engines thrust it forward while air resistance, or drag, tries to slow it down. The wings must produce enough lift to overcome its weight. The diagram on the left shows these four forces.

PITCH, ROLL, YAW

An aircraft can turn in three ways, called pitch, roll and yaw. Raising or lowering its nose is a change in pitch. Lowering one wing and raising the other makes the aircraft roll. Turning the nose to the left or right is a yaw movement. The diagram on the right shows the parts of the aircraft that are operated to make the movements occur.

WING AIRFLOW

Air flowing over the top of a wing has to travel farther and faster than air flowing under it. This makes the air pressure over the wing fall, creating an upward force called lift.

FLAPS AND SLATS

When a plane takes off or lands, slats move out in front of its wings and flaps stretch out behind them. They make the wings bigger to produce more lift when the plane is flying slowly. When it lands, spoilers lift up to "spoil" the wing's shape and reduce lift.

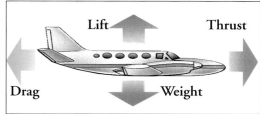

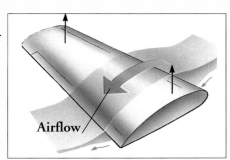

Airflow

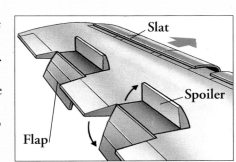

Slat

Spoiler

Flap

JET ENGINE

A spinning fan sucks air inside the engine, where fuel is sprayed into it and lit. The gases rush out of the engine as a jet, which produces thrust.

Roll

Rudder controls yaw

Elevators control pitch

Ailerons control roll

Yaw

Pitch

Lift

HELICOPTER

A helicopter's rotor blades are long, thin wings. As they whirl around, air flowing over them produces a force acting upward. Making the blades spin faster or changing the angle of the blades alters the lifting force. The tail rotor prevents the helicopter itself from being spun around by the action of the main rotor blade.

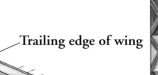

Development and uses of aircraft

The development of aircraft and the speed at which this has happened has been astonishing. Only 66 years separate the very first airplane and supersonic airliners. At first, a variety of purposes were achieved by a single aircraft. For example, the same plane was used for spying and dropping bombs. It became apparent, however, that one aircraft could not carry out different sorts of functions efficiently. Aircraft were therefore designed whose construction suited particular purposes. Nowadays, we have different types of planes, ranging from airliners and planes that spray crops and fight fires to bombers and spyplanes.

TAKING OFF

The chart below shows the key dates in the development of aircraft from the first plane in 1903 to the F-117A high-tech stealth fighter used today.

1940s: Avro Lancaster Bomber: the most successful bomber of World War II

1947: First supersonic flight in a Bell X-1 experimental rocket-powered plane

1930s: First flying boats. These were planes that landed on water.

1936: Igor Sikorsky designed a helicopter with an overhead main rotor and a smaller tail rotor.

1930s: Development of airships. The *Hindenburg* (1936) was the largest of these.

1920s: First commercial airliner: Handley Page HP42

1903: First powered airplane: *Flyer 1*

Harrier AV8-A instrument panel

Flyer 1's controls

Sopwith Camel pilot

"Blackbird" pilot

DEVELOPMENT

Designers have constantly looked for ways of improving their aircraft. Aircraft have become safer, more comfortable and faster. As aircraft have become more specialized, so too has their design. Each new design has provided valuable experience that has led to further improvements.

FLYING CONTROLS

Cables were used to steer early planes. They were linked to the plane's control surfaces and were operated by the pilot. Nowadays, planes are too powerful and fast to be operated manually. In the latest steering system, called fly-by-wire, computers operate the plane's control surfaces.

Sopwith Camel wings

CLOTHING

Clothing worn by pilots has become more specialized. The pilots of early planes wore leather helmets, fleece-lined leather coats, trousers and goggles. Nowadays, pilots who fly at high altitude wear pressure suits and helmets.

Harrier AV8-A engine

Flyer 1 engine

WINGS

The first aircraft had two pairs of wings held in place by wires and wooden struts. As airplane speed increased, the wood and wire caused too much air resistance. Modern aircraft have one pair of metal wings. The wings are swept back to reduce air resistance.

Concorde "delta" wing

ENGINES

The first airplane engines were piston engines, similar to those in a modern car. In the 1930s, Britain and Germany both developed a new type of engine – the jet engine. Jet-engine aircraft can fly higher and faster than piston-engine planes.

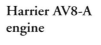

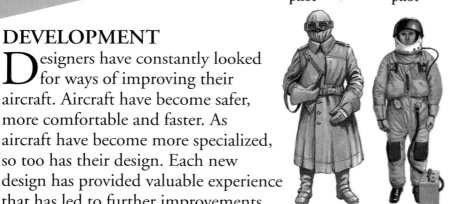

1967: First aircraft capable of vertical takeoff and landing, as well as short takeoff and landing: the Harrier "Jump Jet"

1981: First stealth combat aircraft: Lockheed F-117A "Nighthawk"

1949: First jet airliner: de Havilland Comet. Entered service in 1952

1958: First transatlantic jet airliner services between London and New York with a de Havilland Comet 4

1964: First stealth aircraft: Lockheed SR-71 "Blackbird"

1969: First supersonic airliner: Concorde

USES

Aircraft are used for civilian and military purposes. They transport people and goods from place to place far more quickly than would be possible by road, rail or sea. Military aircraft are used for defense and attack. Some of them are bombers, others are fighters, others are capable of both. Some military aircraft are used for spying. Large numbers of small aircraft are also flown for leisure.

CIVILIAN AIRCRAFT

Vacations in far-away places would be impossible for most people without fast air travel. Business around the world would also be far more difficult. At first, there were very few airports. Airplanes took off from fields. Nowadays, many cities have at least one airport. The picture above shows the boarding walkway leading from the airport terminal to the aircraft.

FLYING FOR FUN

Many different types of aircraft exist that are flown for fun. Examples of these are balloons, single-seat aircraft called microlights, hang-gliders and gliders. Gliders, shown above, are first towed into the sky by another plane or by a winch on the ground, and then use rising columns of air to carry them upward.

MILITARY AIRCRAFT

Winning control of the air is a vital part of winning a war. Fighters patrol the skies ready to attack enemy aircraft. Ground-attack aircraft and bombers strike against targets on the ground. Transport aircraft carry troops, vehicles and supplies to where they are needed and reconnaissance aircraft spy on the enemy. The picture to the right shows a jeep driving out of a Boeing Vertol CH-47 Chinook.

The first flight

"Only those who are acquainted with practical aeronautics can appreciate the difficulties of attempting the first trials of a flying machine in a 25-mile gale . . . but . . . we were determined . . . to know whether the machine possessed sufficient power to fly."
Wilbur Wright's statement to *The Associated Press*, January 5, 1904

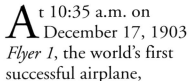

Wilbur Wright   *Orville Wright*

At 10:35 a.m. on December 17, 1903 *Flyer 1*, the world's first successful airplane, accelerated along its launching rail and rose into the air. Twelve seconds later, it landed 100yds. (30m) away on the soft sand at Kill Devil Hills near Kitty Hawk in North Carolina. It was the first time a piloted machine had taken off under its own power and made a controlled flight. The pilot, Orville Wright, and his brother, Wilbur, had built the plane after four years of experiments with kites and gliders. Flying the first airplane was difficult and dangerous. *Flyer 1* had no cockpit or even a seat to sit on! The pilot lay on the lower wing and steered by sliding from side to side. It landed on skids, not wheels.

WRIGHT BROTHERS

The first successful airplanes were designed by two American bicycle makers; Wilbur (1867–1912) and Orville (1871–1948) Wright.

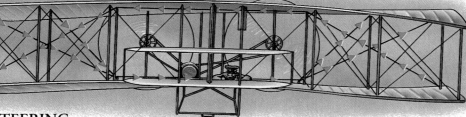

STEERING

Flyer 1 was steered by twisting its wings. The Wright brothers called it wing-warping. The wings were warped, or twisted, by pulling cables attached to them and to the cradle the pilot lay in. The pilot steered by sliding his body to one side or the other.

Upper wing

Bracing wire

TAKEOFF

While one brother piloted the plane, the other brother stayed at the takeoff point and timed the flight with a stopwatch.

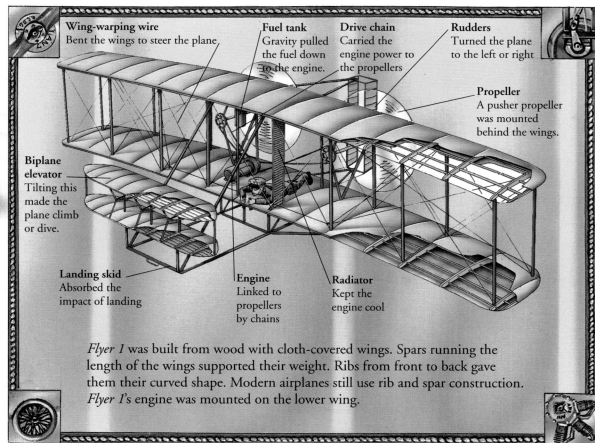

Wing-warping wire
Bent the wings to steer the plane

Fuel tank
Gravity pulled
the fuel down
to the engine.

Drive chain
Carried the
engine power to
the propellers

Rudders
Turned the plane
to the left or right

Propeller
A pusher propeller
was mounted
behind the wings.

Biplane
elevator
Tilting this
made the
plane climb
or dive.

Landing skid
Absorbed the
impact of landing

Engine
Linked to
propellers
by chains

Radiator
Kept the
engine cool

Flyer 1 was built from wood with cloth-covered wings. Spars running the length of the wings supported their weight. Ribs from front to back gave them their curved shape. Modern airplanes still use rib and spar construction. *Flyer 1's* engine was mounted on the lower wing.

ENGINEERING SUCCESS

The brothers designed their own engine because car engines were too heavy and motorcycle engines were not powerful enough. Their engine had four cylinders, weighed 200lb. (90kg) and created 12 hp – about a sixth of the engine power of a small modern car. The plane's top speed was 30mph (48kph).

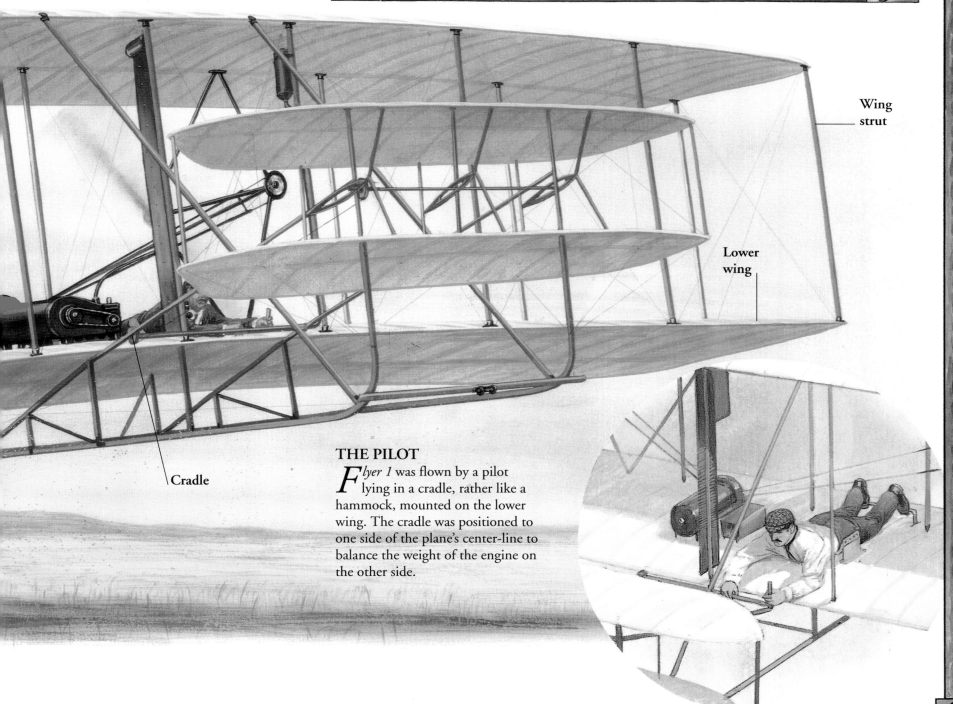

Wing
strut

Lower
wing

Cradle

THE PILOT

Flyer 1 was flown by a pilot lying in a cradle, rather like a hammock, mounted on the lower wing. The cradle was positioned to one side of the plane's center-line to balance the weight of the engine on the other side.

Canvas and string

"The Camel . . . was a death-trap for an inexperienced pilot. Skilled pilots could not wish for a better mount . . . They were wonderful in a dogfight because they could make the quickest change of direction of any machine that flew [in World War I]."

Major W.G. Moore, OBE, DSC, and RNAS pilot

The Sopwith Camel was built during Word War I (1914–1918) as a fighter plane, and was based on the earlier Sopwith Pup fighter. It was one of the greatest fighter aircraft of the war. At a height of 19,028ft. (5,800m) it could reach a speed of 115mph (185kph), and could fly 100mi. (160km) before it needed to be refueled. It could fly for two hours at the most. More than 5,000 were built and they shot down almost 2,800 German planes. The Camels were faster and more maneuverable than most other fighters. But they were difficult to fly. A careless tug on the joystick could send a Camel into a dangerous spin or even throw the pilot out of the cockpit. And during this time, pilots did not wear parachutes! The pilot sat in a wicker seat in front of the fuel tank. His view was restricted by the upper wing and struts.

HAND BOMBING

The Sopwith Camel carried four 24-lb. (11-kg) bombs as well as other weapons. At the beginning of the war, before the introduction of bomb racks and aiming sights, the bombs were dropped from the cockpit by the pilot.

Bracing wire

Upper wing

Rotary engine

Lower wing

Wooden propeller

Metal engine cover

AERIAL PHOTOGRAPHY

Using planes for reconnaissance purposes was a new development in warfare. Sopwith Camel pilots took aerial photographs of enemy territory (1), and the photographs were used to make maps (2). These enabled the pilots to identify targets and the position of enemy troops.

PILOTS' CLOTHING

The air temperature drops very quickly as aircraft climb. Camel pilots had to wear leather helmets and fleece-lined leather clothes on top of thick sweaters, trousers, gloves and socks. Goggles protected the pilots' eyes from cold wind and from oil sprayed out by the engine. By the end of the war, pilots wore one-piece waxed-cotton flying suits lined with silk and fur.

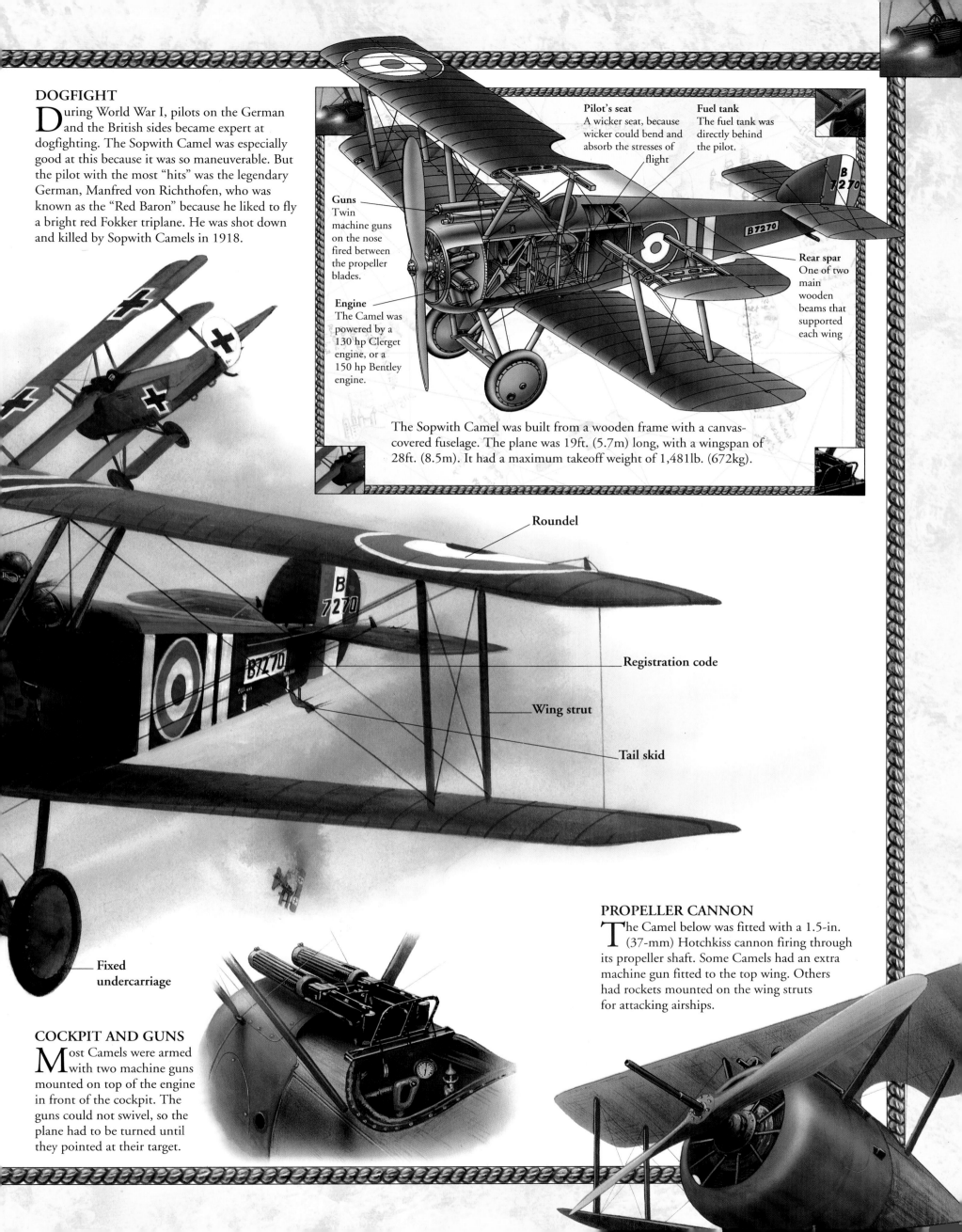

DOGFIGHT

During World War I, pilots on the German and the British sides became expert at dogfighting. The Sopwith Camel was especially good at this because it was so maneuverable. But the pilot with the most "hits" was the legendary German, Manfred von Richthofen, who was known as the "Red Baron" because he liked to fly a bright red Fokker triplane. He was shot down and killed by Sopwith Camels in 1918.

Pilot's seat
A wicker seat, because wicker could bend and absorb the stresses of flight

Fuel tank
The fuel tank was directly behind the pilot.

Guns
Twin machine guns on the nose fired between the propeller blades.

Engine
The Camel was powered by a 130 hp Clerget engine, or a 150 hp Bentley engine.

Rear spar
One of two main wooden beams that supported each wing

The Sopwith Camel was built from a wooden frame with a canvas-covered fuselage. The plane was 19ft. (5.7m) long, with a wingspan of 28ft. (8.5m). It had a maximum takeoff weight of 1,481lb. (672kg).

Roundel

Registration code

Wing strut

Tail skid

Fixed undercarriage

PROPELLER CANNON

The Camel below was fitted with a 1.5-in. (37-mm) Hotchkiss cannon firing through its propeller shaft. Some Camels had an extra machine gun fitted to the top wing. Others had rockets mounted on the wing struts for attacking airships.

COCKPIT AND GUNS

Most Camels were armed with two machine guns mounted on top of the engine in front of the cockpit. The guns could not swivel, so the plane had to be turned until they pointed at their target.

Flying banana

Croydon
Paris
Cairo
Delhi
Cape Town

The Handley Page HP42s were nicknamed "Flying Bananas" because of the curve in their fuselage. They were designed in the late 1920s initially as special air mail planes for the British Imperial Airways airline. The HP42s also met the growing need for commercial passenger planes, and became the world's first airliners. The routes took passengers from Croydon Airport near London to France, India and southern Africa. Only eight of these biplanes were ever built. However, by the time they went out of service in 1940, they had flown a total of 9 million mi. (16 million km) without injuring a single passenger. The HP42s were designed for comfort and safety, not speed. They flew at no more than 94mph (152kph).

CROSSING CONTINENTS

The HP42 flights all took off from Croydon Airport in England. The four-hour journey to France ended at Le Bourget Airport, Paris. The six-day journey to India took passengers around the Mediterranean, through the Persian Gulf and over the sea to Pakistan. Another route flew over the Mediterranean and on to southern Africa. This took eight and a half days.

Wire bracing

Fabric wing-panel covering

Biplane tail

BOARDING PASSENGERS

Passengers boarded the HP42 through a canvas tunnel. As the plane was dedicated to the comfort and convenience of the passengers, the engines were started before they boarded to save time. The tunnel therefore shielded them from the backwash (wind) made by the propellers.

LOADING THE MAIL

Mailbags were loaded on board the HP42 at Croydon Airport. The HP42 was designed as a mail plane because Imperial Airways needed a new plane to carry air mail to India. It was one of the first planes to carry mail on international scheduled air services.

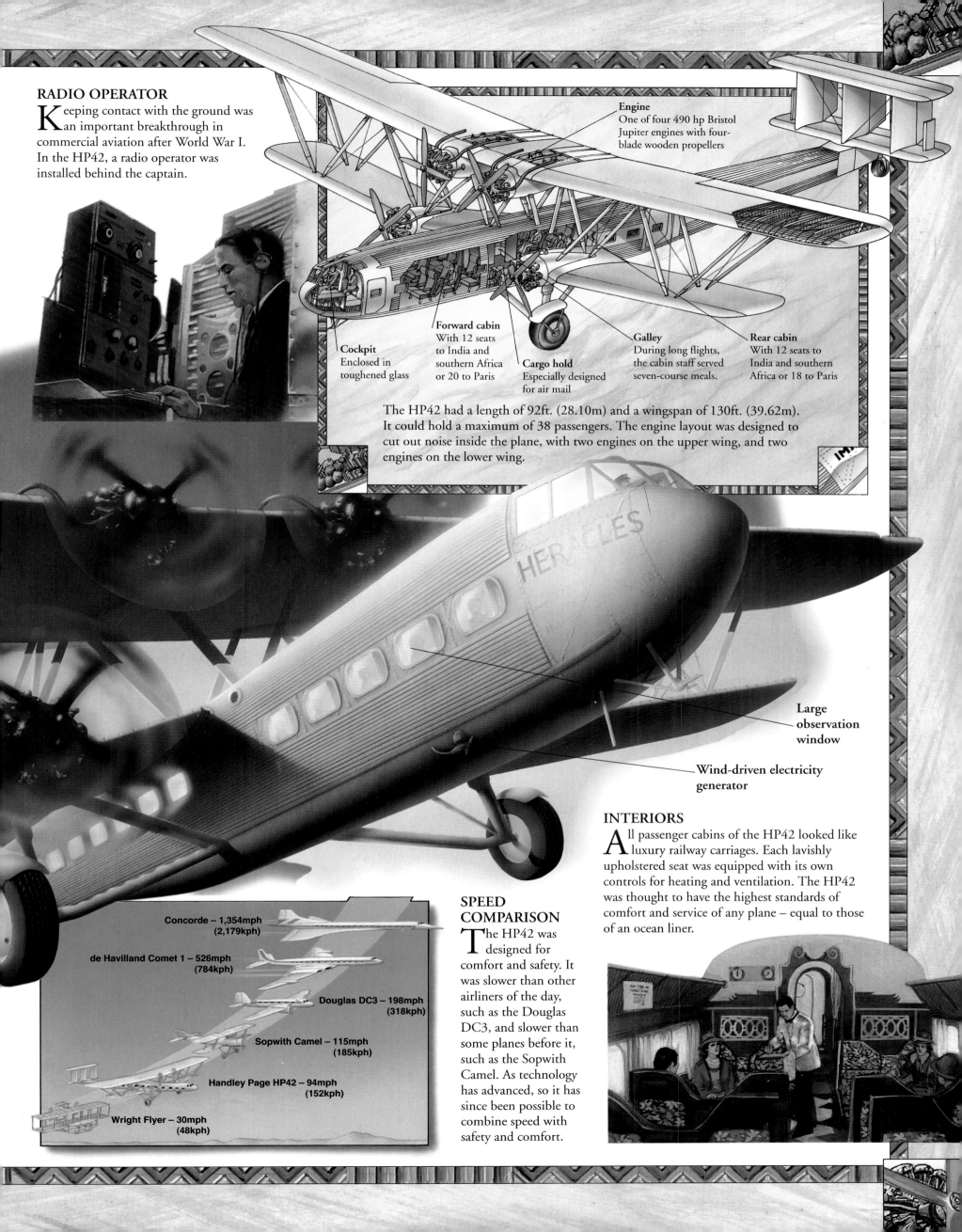

RADIO OPERATOR

Keeping contact with the ground was an important breakthrough in commercial aviation after World War I. In the HP42, a radio operator was installed behind the captain.

Engine
One of four 490 hp Bristol Jupiter engines with four-blade wooden propellers

Cockpit
Enclosed in toughened glass

Forward cabin
With 12 seats to India and southern Africa or 20 to Paris

Cargo hold
Especially designed for air mail

Galley
During long flights, the cabin staff served seven-course meals.

Rear cabin
With 12 seats to India and southern Africa or 18 to Paris

The HP42 had a length of 92ft. (28.10m) and a wingspan of 130ft. (39.62m). It could hold a maximum of 38 passengers. The engine layout was designed to cut out noise inside the plane, with two engines on the upper wing, and two engines on the lower wing.

Large observation window

Wind-driven electricity generator

INTERIORS

All passenger cabins of the HP42 looked like luxury railway carriages. Each lavishly upholstered seat was equipped with its own controls for heating and ventilation. The HP42 was thought to have the highest standards of comfort and service of any plane – equal to those of an ocean liner.

SPEED COMPARISON

The HP42 was designed for comfort and safety. It was slower than other airliners of the day, such as the Douglas DC3, and slower than some planes before it, such as the Sopwith Camel. As technology has advanced, so it has since been possible to combine speed with safety and comfort.

Concorde – 1,354mph (2,179kph)

de Havilland Comet 1 – 526mph (784kph)

Douglas DC3 – 198mph (318kph)

Sopwith Camel – 115mph (185kph)

Handley Page HP42 – 94mph (152kph)

Wright Flyer – 30mph (48kph)

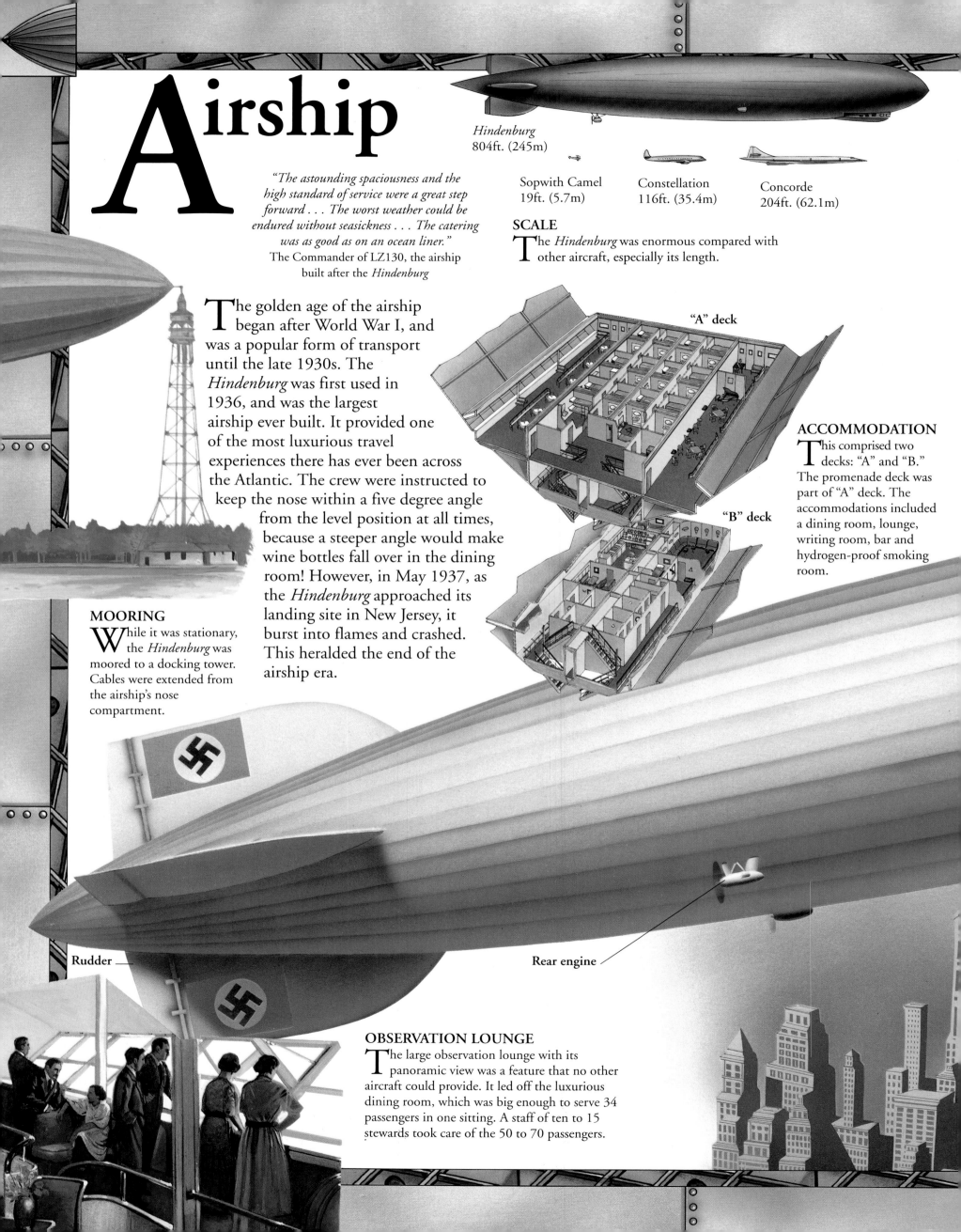

Airship

"The astounding spaciousness and the high standard of service were a great step forward . . . The worst weather could be endured without seasickness . . . The catering was as good as on an ocean liner."
The Commander of LZ130, the airship built after the *Hindenburg*

Hindenburg
804ft. (245m)

Sopwith Camel
19ft. (5.7m)

Constellation
116ft. (35.4m)

Concorde
204ft. (62.1m)

SCALE
The *Hindenburg* was enormous compared with other aircraft, especially its length.

The golden age of the airship began after World War I, and was a popular form of transport until the late 1930s. The *Hindenburg* was first used in 1936, and was the largest airship ever built. It provided one of the most luxurious travel experiences there has ever been across the Atlantic. The crew were instructed to keep the nose within a five degree angle from the level position at all times, because a steeper angle would make wine bottles fall over in the dining room! However, in May 1937, as the *Hindenburg* approached its landing site in New Jersey, it burst into flames and crashed. This heralded the end of the airship era.

"A" deck

"B" deck

ACCOMMODATION
This comprised two decks: "A" and "B." The promenade deck was part of "A" deck. The accommodations included a dining room, lounge, writing room, bar and hydrogen-proof smoking room.

MOORING
While it was stationary, the *Hindenburg* was moored to a docking tower. Cables were extended from the airship's nose compartment.

Rudder

Rear engine

OBSERVATION LOUNGE
The large observation lounge with its panoramic view was a feature that no other aircraft could provide. It led off the luxurious dining room, which was big enough to serve 34 passengers in one sitting. A staff of ten to 15 stewards took care of the 50 to 70 passengers.

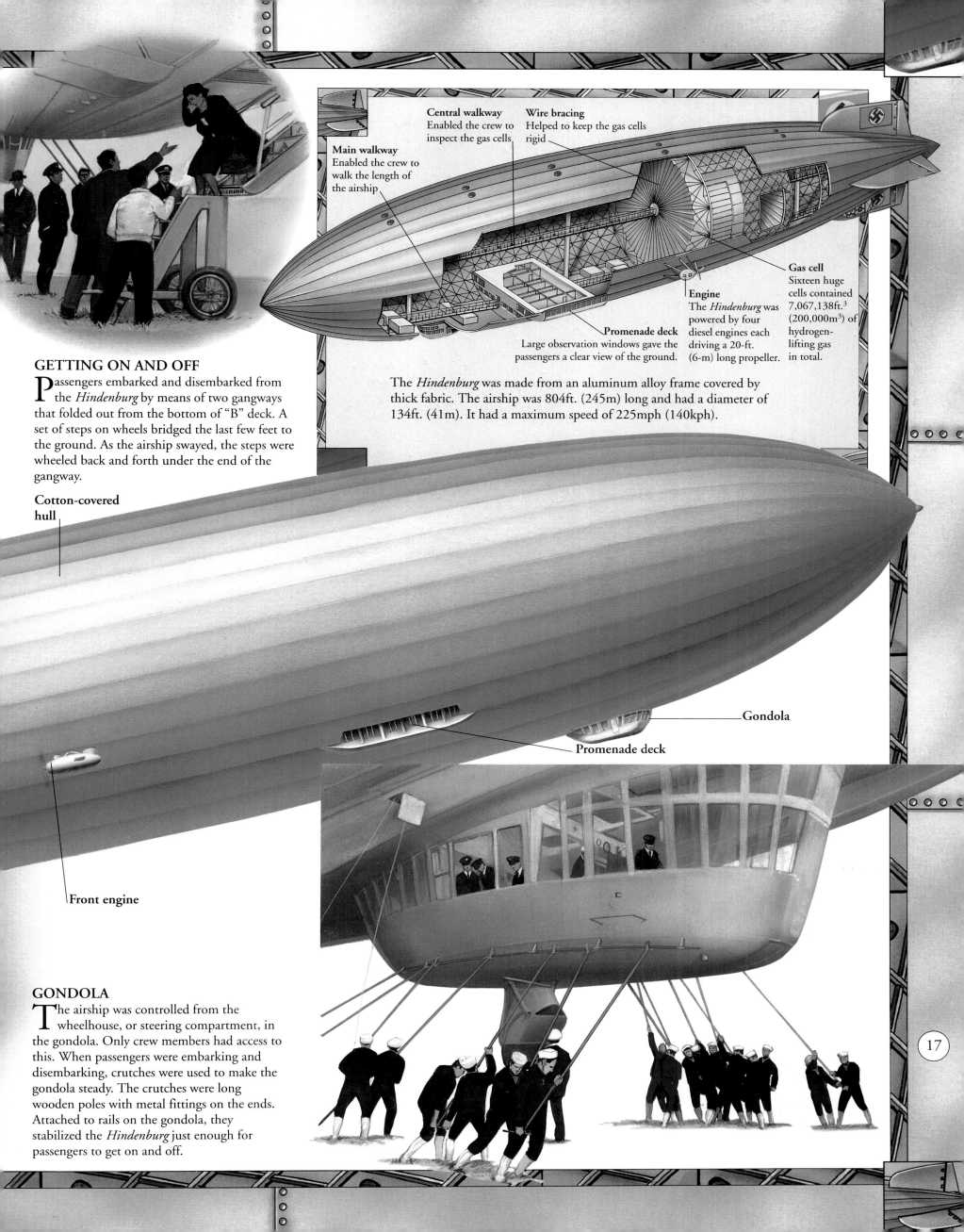

Central walkway
Enabled the crew to
inspect the gas cells

Wire bracing
Helped to keep the gas cells
rigid

Main walkway
Enabled the crew to
walk the length of
the airship

Gas cell
Sixteen huge
cells contained
7,067,138ft.^{3}
(200,000m^3) of
hydrogen-
lifting gas
in total.

Engine
The *Hindenburg* was
powered by four
diesel engines each
driving a 20-ft.
(6-m) long propeller.

Promenade deck
Large observation windows gave the
passengers a clear view of the ground.

The *Hindenburg* was made from an aluminum alloy frame covered by
thick fabric. The airship was 804ft. (245m) long and had a diameter of
134ft. (41m). It had a maximum speed of 225mph (140kph).

GETTING ON AND OFF

Passengers embarked and disembarked from
the *Hindenburg* by means of two gangways
that folded out from the bottom of "B" deck. A
set of steps on wheels bridged the last few feet to
the ground. As the airship swayed, the steps were
wheeled back and forth under the end of the
gangway.

**Cotton-covered
hull**

Gondola

Promenade deck

Front engine

GONDOLA

The airship was controlled from the
wheelhouse, or steering compartment, in
the gondola. Only crew members had access to
this. When passengers were embarking and
disembarking, crutches were used to make the
gondola steady. The crutches were long
wooden poles with metal fittings on the ends.
Attached to rails on the gondola, they
stabilized the *Hindenburg* just enough for
passengers to get on and off.

17

Flying boat

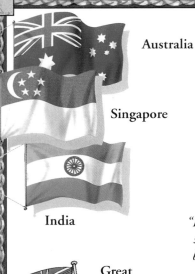

Australia

Singapore

India

Great Britain

"I had a wonderful flight – taking off and landing in water was so smooth and fast! My journey to Marseilles was rather chilly, but the steward brought us blankets and a hot drink. I landed in Australia, two weeks after leaving England, wishing my adventure could begin all over again."
Lady Geraldine Marshall, on her arrival in Australia with Qantas Empire Airways flying boat

Flying boats were developed in the 1930s and were the most comfortable and spacious passenger planes of the time. Their boat-like hulls and under-wing floats enabled them to operate from the sea, lakes and rivers at a time when there were few airports. Flying boats flew all the way to the Far East, making stops in dozens of strange and exotic places and taking about two weeks to get there. The Short S-23 "C" Class Empire flying boat was designed by Short Brothers of Belfast. The first of this class, *Canopus,* had its maiden flight on July 4, 1936. It was bigger, faster and more powerful than other flying boats. It carried airmail bags, light freight and 24 passengers.

FLAGS
When the plane landed and became a boat, it often flew flags in the same way as a boat. The national flags of countries the plane visited or the merchant navy red ensign were raised above the cockpit.

SERVING FOOD
The Empire flying boat was equipped with a galley, or kitchen, where simple meals and drinks were prepared. At a cruising height of 4,920ft. (1,500m), the aircraft could be shaken by sudden rough weather, making it difficult to serve meals and uncomfortable to eat them.

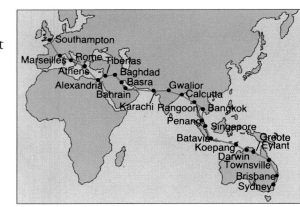

THE EMPIRE ROUTE
Passengers boarded their flying boat at Southampton on the south coast of England. From there, they flew along the route shown on the map (left) to Sydney, Australia. The return fare was almost $400.00.

GETTING ON AND OFF
Passengers boarded their flying boat from a jetty, or floating walkway, to which the plane was moored. In the course of their journey to the other side of the world, they had to make frequent landings so that the plane could be refueled. Each time it touched down, the passengers were taken ashore by launch for a meal or an overnight stay in a nearby hotel.

Navigation light

International identification number

All-metal wing

PROMENADE CABIN

Ocean-going liners often had a promenade deck where passengers could walk around and enjoy the view. The Empire flying boats competed directly with these liners and so they tried to offer a similar level of comfort and facilities. They had a roomy promenade cabin that enabled passengers to walk around and enjoy a spectacular bird's-eye view. They could see the ground below through observation ports.

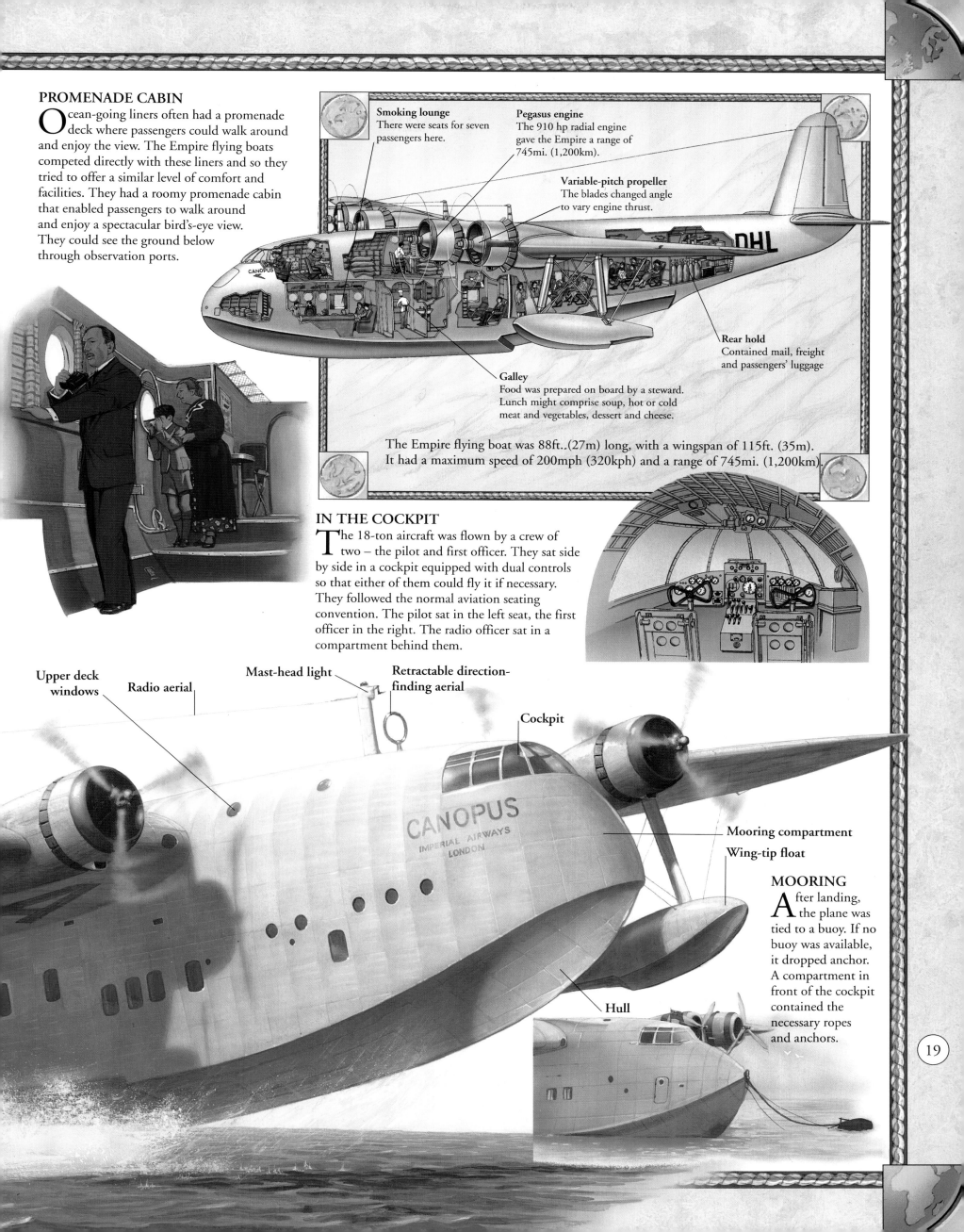

Smoking lounge
There were seats for seven passengers here.

Pegasus engine
The 910 hp radial engine gave the Empire a range of 745mi. (1,200km).

Variable-pitch propeller
The blades changed angle to vary engine thrust.

Rear hold
Contained mail, freight and passengers' luggage

Galley
Food was prepared on board by a steward. Lunch might comprise soup, hot or cold meat and vegetables, dessert and cheese.

The Empire flying boat was 88ft..(27m) long, with a wingspan of 115ft. (35m). It had a maximum speed of 200mph (320kph) and a range of 745mi. (1,200km).

IN THE COCKPIT

The 18-ton aircraft was flown by a crew of two – the pilot and first officer. They sat side by side in a cockpit equipped with dual controls so that either of them could fly it if necessary. They followed the normal aviation seating convention. The pilot sat in the left seat, the first officer in the right. The radio officer sat in a compartment behind them.

Upper deck windows

Radio aerial

Mast-head light

Retractable direction-finding aerial

Cockpit

Mooring compartment

Wing-tip float

CANOPUS
IMPERIAL AIRWAYS
LONDON

MOORING

After landing, the plane was tied to a buoy. If no buoy was available, it dropped anchor. A compartment in front of the cockpit contained the necessary ropes and anchors.

Hull

Timeless transporter

The Douglas DC-3 is the most successful commercial airliner ever built. Since the first one came into service in 1936, more than 13,000 have been produced, and some are still flying today. Each aircraft could carry up to 32 passengers, depending on the seating layout. Although the DC-3 had an unladen weight of 17,703lb. (8,030kg), it could travel at up to 198mph (318kph). The DC-3 entered airline service in 1936 as a sleeper aircraft. It was so successful that by 1939, 90 percent of the world's airline passengers were carried in DC-3s. They were flown by a crew of two, with a stewardess to look after the passengers. Although the DC-3 was built originally as a civilian aircraft, most DC-3s were military versions built during World War II (1939–1945). After the war, these were bought up by airlines. One type of DC-3, the C-47, was called the "Dakota." Since then, all versions have been known as Dakotas.

FLIGHT ATTENDANT

When the DC-3 came into service, uniformed flight attendants, or stewardesses as they were known then, were still a new part of air travel. They replaced the uniformed chefs and waiters that were carried on earlier aircraft. The stewardess shown above is wearing a nurse's uniform to show that she has proper nursing qualifications.

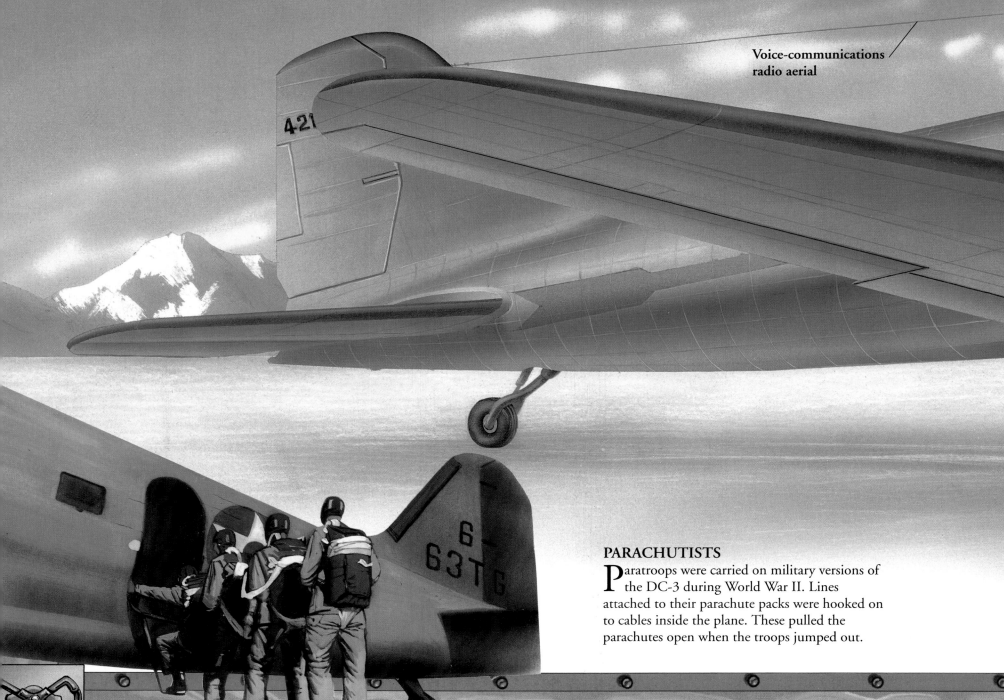

Voice-communications radio aerial

PARACHUTISTS

Paratroops were carried on military versions of the DC-3 during World War II. Lines attached to their parachute packs were hooked on to cables inside the plane. These pulled the parachutes open when the troops jumped out.

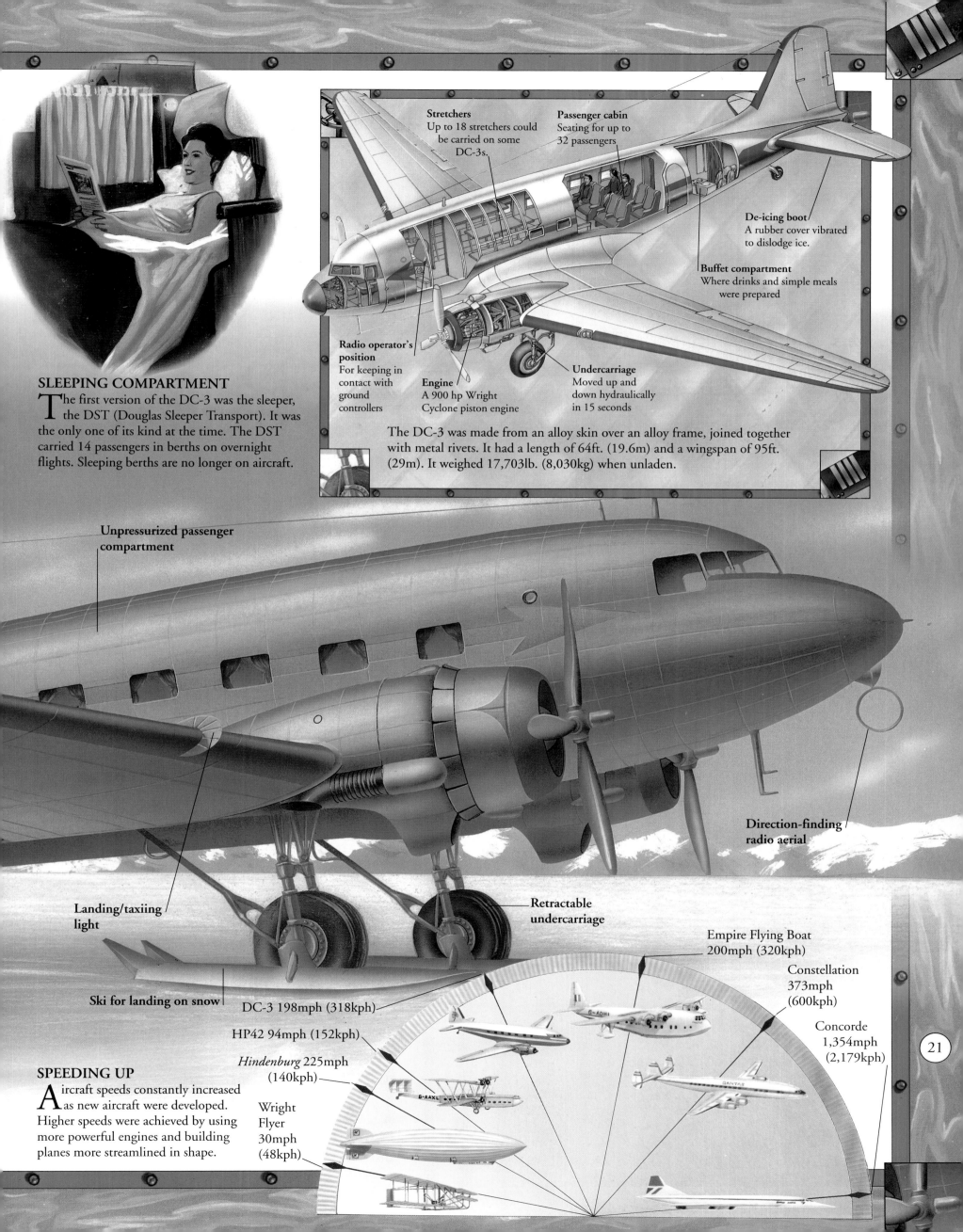

Stretchers
Up to 18 stretchers could
be carried on some
DC-3s.

Passenger cabin
Seating for up to
32 passengers

De-icing boot
A rubber cover vibrated
to dislodge ice.

Buffet compartment
Where drinks and simple meals
were prepared

Radio operator's position
For keeping in
contact with
ground
controllers

Engine
A 900 hp Wright
Cyclone piston engine

Undercarriage
Moved up and
down hydraulically
in 15 seconds

The DC-3 was made from an alloy skin over an alloy frame, joined together
with metal rivets. It had a length of 64ft. (19.6m) and a wingspan of 95ft.
(29m). It weighed 17,703lb. (8,030kg) when unladen.

SLEEPING COMPARTMENT

The first version of the DC-3 was the sleeper,
the DST (Douglas Sleeper Transport). It was
the only one of its kind at the time. The DST
carried 14 passengers in berths on overnight
flights. Sleeping berths are no longer on aircraft.

**Unpressurized passenger
compartment**

**Direction-finding
radio aerial**

**Landing/taxiing
light**

**Retractable
undercarriage**

Ski for landing on snow

Empire Flying Boat
200mph (320kph)

Constellation
373mph
(600kph)

DC-3 198mph (318kph)

Concorde
1,354mph
(2,179kph)

HP42 94mph (152kph)

Hindenburg 225mph
(140kph)

Wright
Flyer
30mph
(48kph)

SPEEDING UP

Aircraft speeds constantly increased
as new aircraft were developed.
Higher speeds were achieved by using
more powerful engines and building
planes more streamlined in shape.

21

A fearsome fighter

"The fastest aircraft to fly before World War II was a special development of the German Messerschmitt Bf109 . . . setting a record that was not beaten by another piston-engined airplane until 30 years later."
Michael Taylor and David Mondey, *Guinness Book of Aircraft, Facts and Feats*, 1970

The German Messerschmitt Bf109 was developed in the 1930s by Willy Messerschmitt. It became one of the fastest, most maneuverable and well-armed fighters of World War II. Approximately 35,000 were built – more than any other fighter. It had a special system for supplying fuel to the engine, enabling it to perform maneuvers which were impossible for other aircraft. The fastest version of the Bf109 could fly at up to 398mph (640kph) and could reach a maximum height of 36,090ft. (11,000m). It was a very popular aircraft with German pilots. They flew it high and fast, ready to accelerate to combat-speed and pounce on enemy fighters, or sweep down to attack slow-flying bombers. The Bf109's main fault was that it could not carry much fuel. It could only fly 410mi. (660km) without refueling. With such a short range, the plane was not able to linger for very long in the important combat zone over southern England.

GROUND WAR ROOM

The routes of German bombers and their fighter escorts, which protected them, were plotted on a map in the huge Berlin war room. The commanders then knew exactly how many aircraft were in action, and their positions. Many escorts were made up of Bf109s. German bomber crews believed that the Bf109s protected them more effectively than any other fighter aircraft.

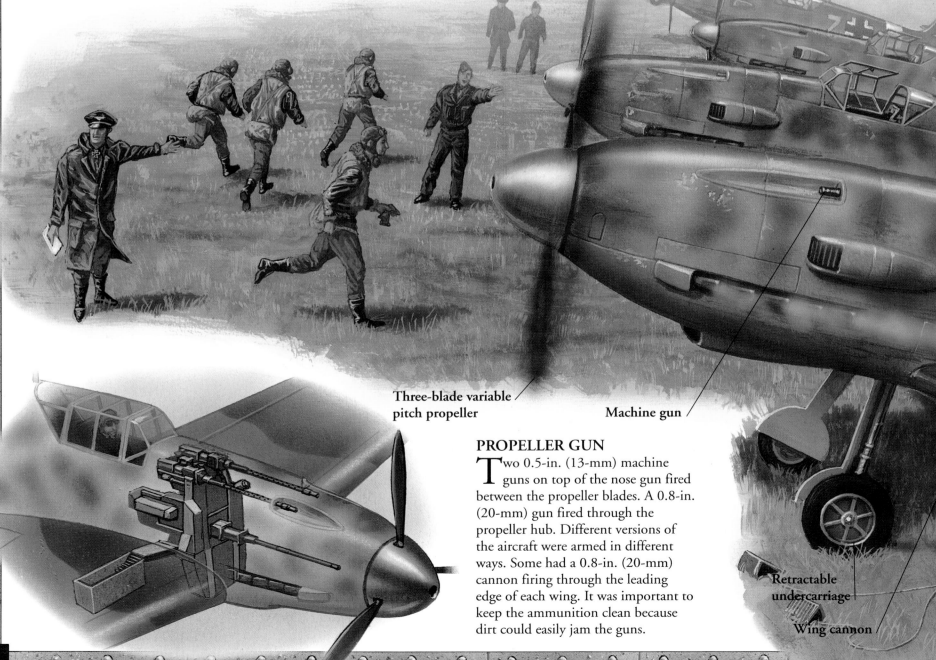

Three-blade variable pitch propeller

Machine gun

PROPELLER GUN

Two 0.5-in. (13-mm) machine guns on top of the nose gun fired between the propeller blades. A 0.8-in. (20-mm) gun fired through the propeller hub. Different versions of the aircraft were armed in different ways. Some had a 0.8-in. (20-mm) cannon firing through the leading edge of each wing. It was important to keep the ammunition clean because dirt could easily jam the guns.

Retractable undercarriage

Wing cannon

Engine
A Daimler-Benz
DB601A piston
engine

Tailplane handwheel
Changed the angle of
the tailplane to make
the nose tilt up or
down

Fuel tank
Provided
the aircraft with a range
of approximately
410mi. (660km)

Camouflage coloring
For desert warfare

Transmitter/receiver radio pack
To communicate with ground
crew and aircrew

Supercharger
Forced more air
into the engine
to increase
power

Wing cannon
A 0.8-in. (20-mm)
cannon fired through the
leading edge of the wing.

The Bf109 was a streamlined, all-metal monoplane. It was 29ft. (8.85m)
long, with a wingspan of 32ft. (9.9m). It had an unladen weight of 6,834lb.
(3,100kg) and flew up to 398mph (640kph).

COCKPIT

All cockpits in fighter aircraft are small, but
the Bf109's cockpit was especially cramped.
The instrument-panel layout was confusing. The
instruments that were used most frequently were
not in the easiest position for the pilot to see.
The foot pedals on the Bf109's cockpit floor
controlled the plane's rudder. A thick cockpit
frame restricted the pilot's view.

FIGHTER PLANE NUMBERS

During World War II,
almost 100,000
British and German fighter
aircraft were built. The
graph to the right shows
which fighters were built,
and how many
of them.

Messerschmitt Bf110   6,000

Hawker Hurricane   14,000

Focke-Wulf 190 20,000

Spitfire   20,000

Messerschmitt Bf109 35,000

British Royal Air Force 34,000

German Air Force 61,000

Hinged canopy

Radio aerial

Bombs away

"The Lancaster was a thoroughbred. It looked magnificent on the ground – strong and well-proportioned. And it was powerful and well-balanced in the air. The ground crews worked their hearts out to keep us flying. The riggers and fitters, the electricians, mechanics and armorers, they all took a pride in their aircraft."
Norman Mitchell, a Lancaster bomb aimer

MISSION MARKERS

Bomber crews kept a tally of the number of missions they flew by painting a bomb on the aircraft's nose for each mission, which was called a sortie. This Lancaster has flown 47 sorties. Some flew more than 100. Most missions took place at night, when enemy fighter planes could not operate so successfully.

EMBLEMS

Each bomber crew tried to make its aircraft a little different from all the others. They gave the aircraft a name and painted a colorful emblem on its nose. This one shows a lion (a symbol of Britain) eating a German flag.

The British Avro Lancaster was one of the most successful heavy bombers of World War II. More than 7,300 were built. It flew 156,318 bombing missions, and dropped a total of 618,000 tons of bombs. It could carry a heavier bomb, and at a higher altitude, than any similar aircraft and was very maneuverable for its large size. Flying a Lancaster was a physically demanding job. The crew flew to an altitude of 21,982 ft. (6,700m) for up to 12 hours. They had to breathe oxygen through a face mask often in temperatures as low as 23°F (-5°C). The Lancasters rarely had fighter escorts, and flew mostly at night to avoid being attacked.

Mid-upper gun turret

Rear-gun turret

Twin-fin tail

PG

BOMB LOADING

Heavy bombs were driven to a Lancaster on a train of trailers pulled by a tractor. The bombs were then lifted up on to racks inside the bomb bay. The 33-ft. (10-m) long bomb bay could carry different bomb loads. When loaded, the plane took a long time to take off due to the weight.

BOMB STATISTICS

As the war progressed, larger bombs were produced. The doors of the bomb bay were therefore adapted so that they curved outward to carry the bombs.

992lb. (450kg)

2,910lb. (1,320kg) "Bouncing bomb"

8,025lb. (3,640kg) "Blockbuster"

12,014lb. (5,450kg) "Tallboy"

22,046lb. (10,000kg) "Grand Slam"

FLIGHT PLANS AND LOG BOOKS

About three hours before a mission, the crew attended a briefing where they were told what their target for that night was to be. The outward and return routes were plotted on a map, or flight plan. Pilots kept a careful record of all their missions in a log book.

Engine
One of four 1,460 hp Rolls-Royce Merlin piston engines

Tail guns
Four machine guns protected the aircraft's tail.

Ammunition boxes
Supplied ammunition to the gun turrets

Fuel tanks
These enabled the plane to fly 1,730mi. (2,784km) with a bomb load of 12,000lb. (5,443kg).

Machine guns
Two 0.3-in. (7.7-mm) machine guns in nose turret

Dark underside camouflage
Helped conceal the plane from the ground on night-flying missions

Bomb aimer's position
Bomb aimer also fired the front gun

The Lancaster had a length of 70ft. (21.2m), a wingspan of 102ft. (31.1m), and a maximum takeoff weight of 72,000lb. (32,659kg). Its powerful Rolls-Royce Merlin engines gave it a maximum speed of 286mph (460kph) at a height of 21,982ft. (6,700m).

Camouflage colors

LANCASTER CREW

The Lancaster had a crew of seven. They wore up to seven layers of clothing to keep warm during the flight.

1. Wireless operator 2. Front gunner/bomb aimer 3. Flight engineer 4. Navigator 5. Pilot 6. Central gunner 7. Rear gunner

Front-gun turret

Bomb aimer's window

Bomb bay (open)

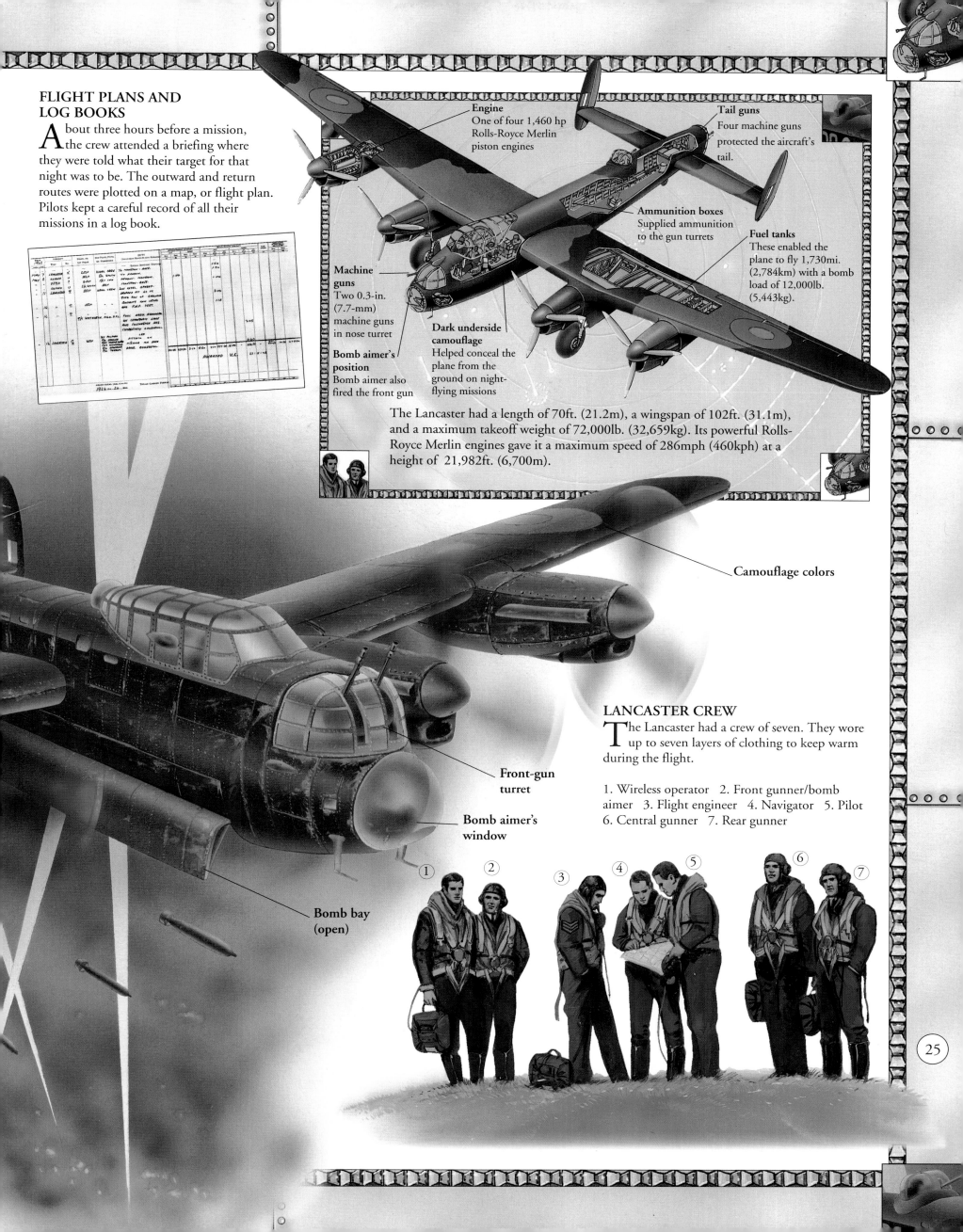

Queen of the airways

"The Constellations have more new features than any other airliner in a decade. They add up to greater speed, a higher degree of safety, more comfort and bigger and better menus."
Norman Ellison, *Sydney Sun*, 1947

The Lockheed Constellation was first developed in 1938 as a commercial airliner, but the planes were taken over by the United States Army during World War II. After the war, the Constellation was developed as a long-haul airliner for commercial flights. It was the first of the post-war airliners and was extensively developed to make long flights more attractive with its extra passenger comfort. Over the years there were many improvements on the first type of Constellation, although its drooping nose and upswept tail remained the same. Super Constellations developed, which had a fuselage that was longer, but a wingspan that remained the same. After this, came "Starliners". These had a fuselage and wings that were longer than those of the Super Constellation. Inside the aircraft, each version of the Constellation introduced new standards in passenger service. A comfortable reclining sleeper seat was first used in an Air Ceylon Constellation in 1956. The elegant Constellation was used until the late 1970s. The aircraft shown on the right is the 1049G, which was a Super Constellation. There were 26 versions of the Constellation and 49 versions of the Super Constellation.

TRANSCONTINENTAL ROUTES

The Constellation helped to open the post-war long-range air routes. Transcontinental services began in 1946 with flights between New York and Bournemouth, and London and Rio de Janeiro.

Triple-fin tail

Upswept tail

De-icing strip

Wing-tip fuel tank

RADAR

In the 1950s the first Super Constellations used in the United States Air Force were transferred from the navy and refitted with a rotating radar dish called a rotodome, shown above. Airborne radar detects enemy planes further away than radar on the ground.

LANDING GEAR

Almost all airliners before the Constellation had a main wheel under each wing and one under the tail. The Constellation had a "tricycle" undercarriage; the wheels were arranged with one at the front and one under each wing, so the passenger cabin was parallel to the ground.

COCKTAIL LOUNGE

Lockheed spent $1,500,000.00 and 120,000 working hours giving the Super Constellation the most luxurious interior of any large passenger aircraft. The cocktail lounge had special lighting effects and peaceful color schemes to make it more relaxing.

Sleeping berths
Constellations could be fitted with up to 22 sleeping berths.

Turbo-compound engine
Four 3,250 hp turbo-supercharged engines powered the "Starliner" and Super Constellation. The first Constellations were powered by 2,300 hp piston engines.

Nosewheel
Retracted backward up into the nose

Main undercarriage
Retracted forward up into the wings

The Constellation shown here is a 1649A, also known as the "Starliner." The Constellation was 95ft. (29m) long, with a wingspan of 123ft. (37.5m). Super Constellations were 114ft. (34.6m) long with a wingspan of 123ft. (37.5m). This "Starliner" model was 116ft. (35.4m) long with a wingspan of 150ft. (45.7m). It had a maximum speed of 373mph (600kph).

Wright R-3350 Turbo-compound engine

SPEEDPAK

The Constellation could not carry much luggage. Lockheed solved this by designing a freight container, called a Speedpak, which could be attached to the aircraft's belly. A built-in electric hoist lowered the Speedpak to the ground for loading and unloading. It doubled the amount of luggage that could be loaded on to the Constellation.

Higher and faster

GALLEY

During the flight, two stewards and a stewardess served meals and drinks. They prepared refreshments in a small galley situated just behind the flight deck. Galleys were not new to passenger aircraft. However, in-flight services became more important with the development of jet airliners.

"The Comet was years ahead of the competition, pioneering jet transportation high above the weather, and achieving journey times half that expected with piston-engined aircraft."
Philip J. Birtles, *Classic Civil Aircraft 3: de Havilland Comet*, 1993

Research into faster military aircraft during World War II speeded up the development of jet engines. At the end of the war, work began on developing jet airliners. The first jet airliner to enter service was the British de Havilland Comet 1 in 1952. It was popular with passengers because it was able to fly higher and faster than any piston-engined airliner. Shorter flights to faraway places, higher above stormy weather, were less tiring and stressful for the passengers. Comets could reach Singapore in 25 hours, or Tokyo in 36 hours. These journeys would have taken almost twice as long in a Super Constellation! But the Comet 1 had its problems, from which all aircraft manufacturers learned. The aircraft was grounded in 1954 after a series of crashes. Investigators found that the greater difference in air pressure between the inside and outside of the high-flying airplane put extra stress on the fuselage, which eventually cracked open in flight. The aircraft was strengthened and enlarged as the Comet 4, shown here, which entered service in 1958.

STRESS ANALYSIS

Following three crashes of the Comet, scientists searched for any fault that might have caused the accidents. The scientists had a Comet sealed inside a pressurized water tank to simulate the stresses of flight. In tests, the fuselage cracked open. The Comet's fuselage was strengthened and the problem ended.

Radio aerial (inside top of tail fin)

Pressurized passenger cabin

Rudder

Instrument Landing System aerial (inside tips of tail plane)

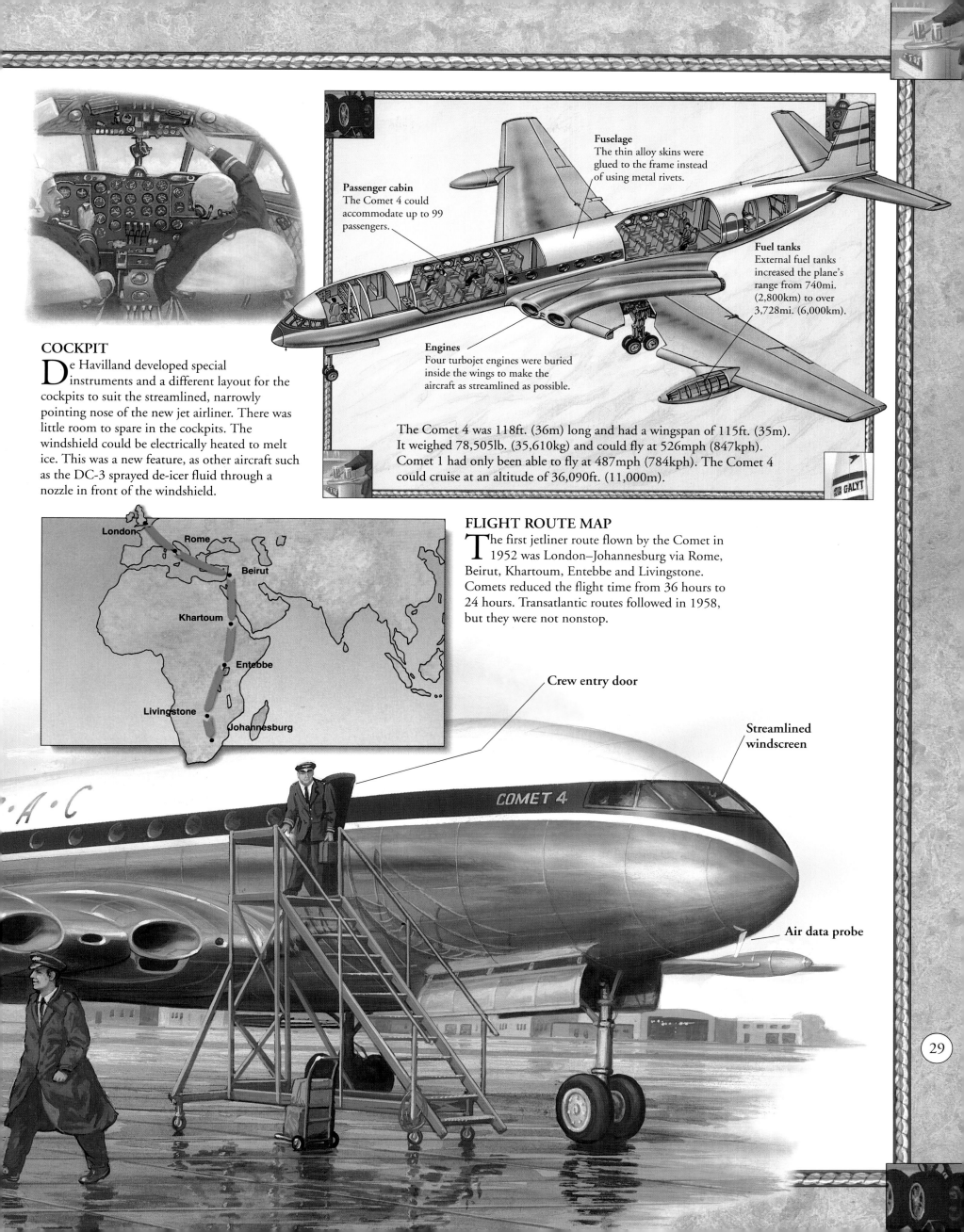

Passenger cabin
The Comet 4 could accommodate up to 99 passengers.

Fuselage
The thin alloy skins were glued to the frame instead of using metal rivets.

Fuel tanks
External fuel tanks increased the plane's range from 740mi. (2,800km) to over 3,728mi. (6,000km).

Engines
Four turbojet engines were buried inside the wings to make the aircraft as streamlined as possible.

The Comet 4 was 118ft. (36m) long and had a wingspan of 115ft. (35m). It weighed 78,505lb. (35,610kg) and could fly at 526mph (847kph). Comet 1 had only been able to fly at 487mph (784kph). The Comet 4 could cruise at an altitude of 36,090ft. (11,000m).

COCKPIT

De Havilland developed special instruments and a different layout for the cockpits to suit the streamlined, narrowly pointing nose of the new jet airliner. There was little room to spare in the cockpits. The windshield could be electrically heated to melt ice. This was a new feature, as other aircraft such as the DC-3 sprayed de-icer fluid through a nozzle in front of the windshield.

FLIGHT ROUTE MAP

The first jetliner route flown by the Comet in 1952 was London–Johannesburg via Rome, Beirut, Khartoum, Entebbe and Livingstone. Comets reduced the flight time from 36 hours to 24 hours. Transatlantic routes followed in 1958, but they were not nonstop.

London
Rome
Beirut
Khartoum
Entebbe
Livingstone
Johannesburg

Crew entry door

Streamlined windscreen

COMET 4

Air data probe

Mighty monster

"Loading and preflight checks took 45 minutes. We normally took a ten-minute break before engine start to get the sweat out of our suits or we'd freeze at altitude."
Captain Don Jansky, B-52 pilot

The American B-52 Stratofortress was first designed in the mid-1940s as a heavy bomber. It developed in the 1950s as a long-range nuclear bomber because World War II had shown that the long-range heavy bomber was the most threatening weapon available to attack an enemy's territory. The huge aircraft is known affectionately by its crews as the "Buff," the Big Ugly Fat Fella. It has never dropped a nuclear bomb, but it has been used for non-nuclear bombing.

Its crew enters the aircraft through a small hatch in its belly. The aircraft commander and copilot fly the plane from their side-by-side seats in the cockpit. Behind them, facing backward, sits the defensive team of electronic warfare officers. One of them also operates the tail gun.

Early B-52 crews wore an uncomfortable skin-tight pressure suit. It inflated automatically if the cabin pressure was lost. Later, B-52s were flown at much lower altitudes to avoid detection by enemy radar. Pressure suits then became unnecessary.

The "Buff" has lasted a long time because it has been updated regularly. Different versions of the latest model of the B-52 exist, including reconnaissance versions. The B-52 can hold many different combinations of weapons. It is the world's heaviest bomber, and can carry up to 99,206lb. (45,000kg) of bombs.

TAIL GUN

The B-52's only defensive armament has been in its tail. The model shown here has a six-barrelled machine gun. Early models were armed with four machine guns.

Turbofan engines

Stratotanker

REFUELING

In-flight refueling means that the B-52 can travel virtually any distance. Lights underneath the tanker aircraft guide the B-52 into the correct position for refueling.

ENGINE

All B-52 Stratofortresses except for the latest model, the B-52H, were powered by eight turbojets, grouped in four pairs. The B-52H is powered by eight turbofans, like the one shown here, because these are quieter and use less fuel than turbojets. They also increase power performance dramatically, allowing the aircraft to take off quickly. These engines can run for 4,000 hours before needing a service – the older turbojets could run for only 500 hours between services.

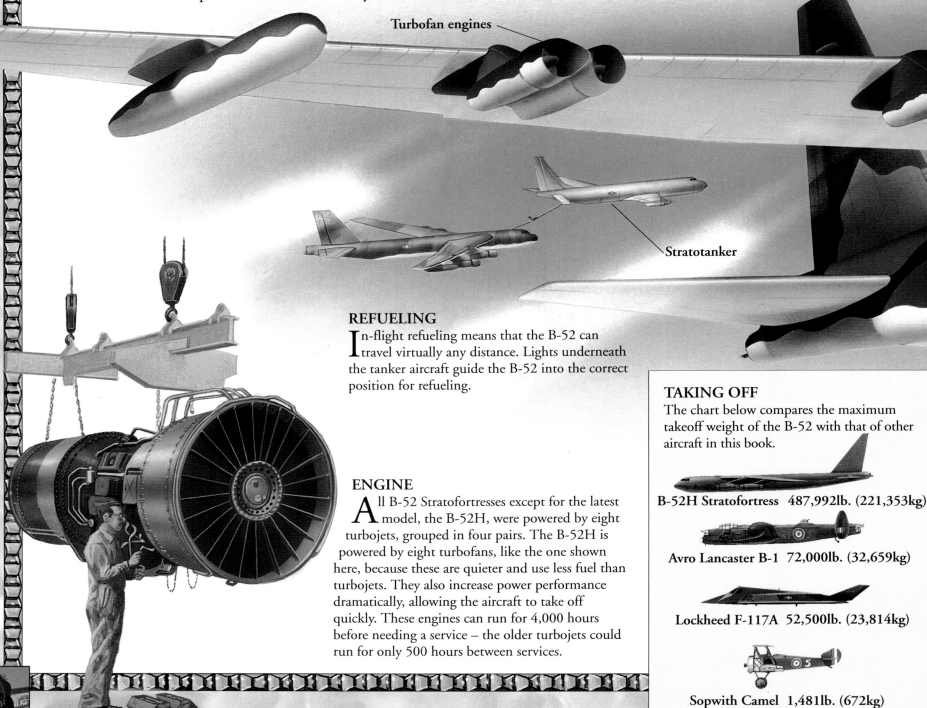

TAKING OFF

The chart below compares the maximum takeoff weight of the B-52 with that of other aircraft in this book.

B-52H Stratofortress 487,992lb. (221,353kg)

Avro Lancaster B-1 72,000lb. (32,659kg)

Lockheed F-117A 52,500lb. (23,814kg)

Sopwith Camel 1,481lb. (672kg)

NAVIGATION

The two radar navigators sit behind and below the cockpit, facing forward. They are beneath the electronic warfare officers. Their seats eject downward through the belly of the aircraft.

Bomb bay
Reconnaissance B-52s carry cameras in their bomb bays.

Entry and exit hatch
Crew enter and leave the aircraft through this.

Engine
One of eight 17,019lb. (7,720kg) Pratt and Whitney turbofans

Outrigger wheel
Supports the wing tips when the aircraft is on the ground

Main wheels
Swivel up into fuselage after takeoff

Tail fin
A narrow rudder runs the full height of the huge tail fin.

The B-52H has a very strong internal structure to support its engines and wings full of fuel. Its maximum speed is 595mph (958kph) at a height of 55,774ft. (17,000m). The plane has a length of 161ft. (49.04m) and weighs up to 487,992lb. (221,353kg) at takeoff.

Low-light television camera

Forward Looking Infra-Red (FLIR) viewing system

Under-wing fuel tank

LOADING MISSILES

Cruise missiles are loaded on to pylons under a B-52's wings. Once they are safely loaded, their explosive warheads are plugged into the empty bays at the front of the missiles.

Whirlybird

"By 1969 American Army Chinooks had flown a total of half a million hours – more than two thirds of them under combat conditions in Korea . . . The Chinook forms part of America's heavy brigade."
Robert Jackson, *The Dragonflies* 1971

The first helicopters were not very strong and could not carry a heavy load, so they were not suited to military requirements. But in the 1950s, the Boeing-Vertol CH-47 Chinook answered the American Army's need for a very powerful helicopter. It had to be one that could transport at least 40 troops and carry a two-ton load inside it. The helicopter also had to be able to fly with an eight-ton load slung underneath it. The Chinook can do this and more. It has become a valuable multipurpose air-truck for transporting troops and equipment. Military forces all over the world use this helicopter. Two sets of controls allow either the pilot or copilot, sitting side by side, to fly the aircraft. The Chinook, like most modern helicopters, is powered by turboshaft jet engines. These are fitted at the rear of the aircraft and linked to the rotor blades by spinning shafts. Noise and vibration from the rotor blades are so great that the crew talk to each other through intercoms.

Rear rotor

Textron Lycoming T55-L-712 turboshaft engine

Radio aerial

US ARMY 981143

ARMY

Cargo ramp

Main cargo hook

LOADING RAMP

With the rear loading ramp lowered, vehicles can be driven straight into and out of the helicopter. The Chinook can move small vehicles quickly by air to wherever they are needed.

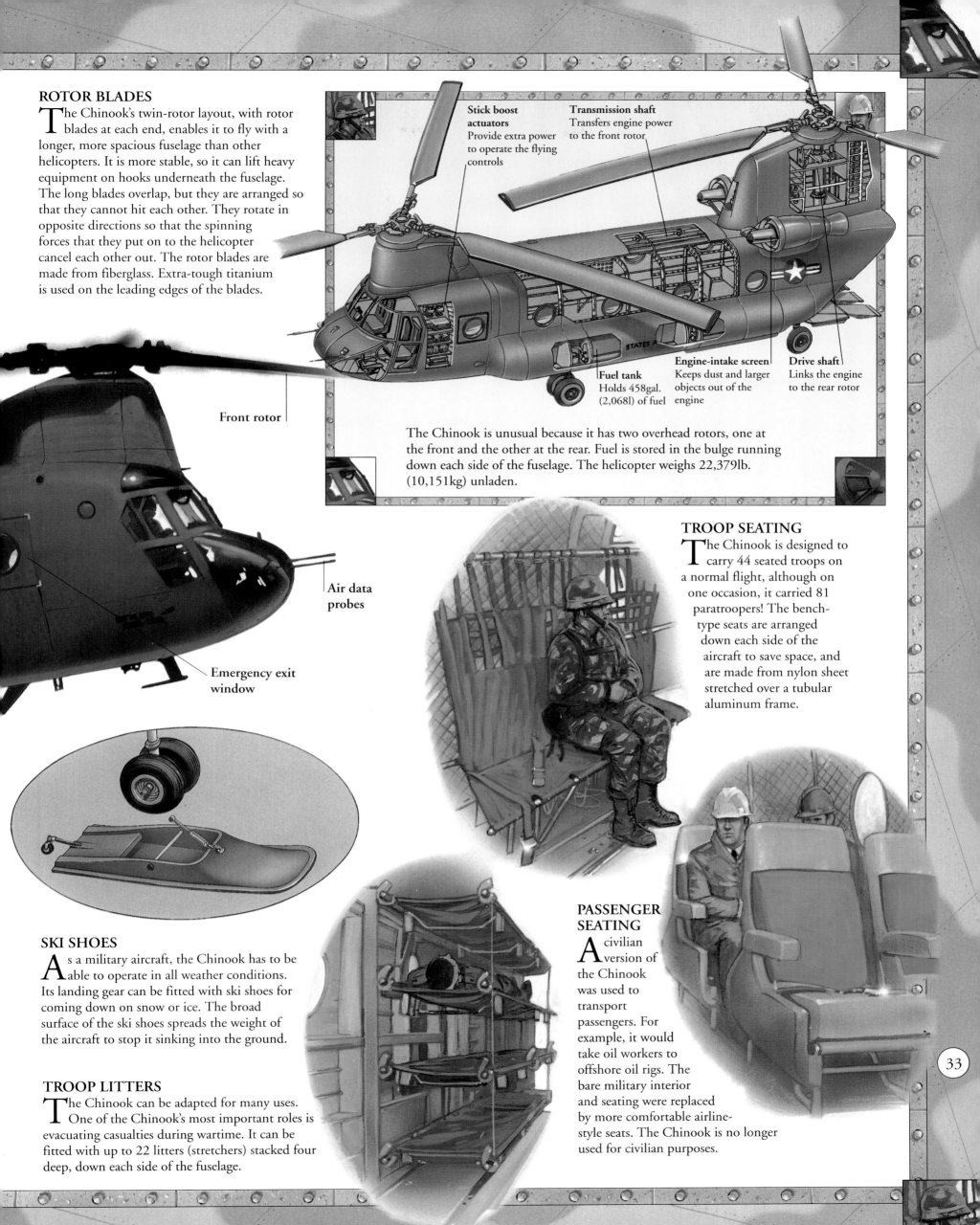

ROTOR BLADES

The Chinook's twin-rotor layout, with rotor blades at each end, enables it to fly with a longer, more spacious fuselage than other helicopters. It is more stable, so it can lift heavy equipment on hooks underneath the fuselage. The long blades overlap, but they are arranged so that they cannot hit each other. They rotate in opposite directions so that the spinning forces that they put on to the helicopter cancel each other out. The rotor blades are made from fiberglass. Extra-tough titanium is used on the leading edges of the blades.

Stick boost actuators
Provide extra power to operate the flying controls

Transmission shaft
Transfers engine power to the front rotor

Fuel tank
Holds 458gal. (2,068l) of fuel

Engine-intake screen
Keeps dust and larger objects out of the engine

Drive shaft
Links the engine to the rear rotor

The Chinook is unusual because it has two overhead rotors, one at the front and the other at the rear. Fuel is stored in the bulge running down each side of the fuselage. The helicopter weighs 22,379lb. (10,151kg) unladen.

Front rotor

Air data probes

Emergency exit window

TROOP SEATING

The Chinook is designed to carry 44 seated troops on a normal flight, although on one occasion, it carried 81 paratroopers! The bench-type seats are arranged down each side of the aircraft to save space, and are made from nylon sheet stretched over a tubular aluminum frame.

SKI SHOES

As a military aircraft, the Chinook has to be able to operate in all weather conditions. Its landing gear can be fitted with ski shoes for coming down on snow or ice. The broad surface of the ski shoes spreads the weight of the aircraft to stop it sinking into the ground.

TROOP LITTERS

The Chinook can be adapted for many uses. One of the Chinook's most important roles is evacuating casualties during wartime. It can be fitted with up to 22 litters (stretchers) stacked four deep, down each side of the fuselage.

PASSENGER SEATING

A civilian version of the Chinook was used to transport passengers. For example, it would take oil workers to offshore oil rigs. The bare military interior and seating were replaced by more comfortable airline-style seats. The Chinook is no longer used for civilian purposes.

Spyplane

"The windscreen gets so hot that a pilot can't keep his hand on it for more than 20 seconds even with flame-retardant gloves."
Captain Thomas L. Peterson, Blackbird pilot

The Lockheed SR-71 entered service in the 1960s as a high-altitude, ultra-fast spyplane. It is the world's first stealth aircraft, and holds the world air-speed record of 2,193mph (3,529kph). It flies at an altitude of 85,300ft. (26,000m), higher than most other aircraft. But more than this, the SR-71 can avoid detection on enemy radar screens because of its black, radar-absorbent paint and its unique shape. Its color has earned the SR-71 the name "Blackbird."

The preparations for each flight begin with two hours of preflight checks. While the aircrew, the pilot and a reconnaissance (spying) systems operator (RSO), put on their pressure suits, the ground crew starts up all the aircraft's systems – from electricity generators and computers to life-support systems. The crew climbs into the cramped cockpit nearly an hour before takeoff. At its maximum speed, its cameras photograph 100,000sq. mi. (259,000sq. km) of the ground every hour.

PRESSURE SUIT

Blackbirds fly at such great altitude that their pilots wear pressure suits and helmets similar to an astronaut's spacesuit. The suit completely seals the pilot inside. The suit has to be supplied with oxygen for the pilot to breathe.

Angled tail fin

Corrugated wing panel

Ejector flap to control exhaust airflow

Main sensor bay

SPY PHOTOS

Despite the speed at which it flies, clear photographs can be taken from Blackbird on its spy missions by panoramic and long-range cameras held in the main sensor bay. The picture above was taken on a practice flight and shows the Los Angeles coastline in California.

PARACHUTE

The Blackbird needs some help to stop from its touchdown speed of 173mph (278kph). A compartment in the top of the fuselage opens and a huge parachute streams out. The drag this creates slows the Blackbird to a halt within about 3,280ft. (1,000m).

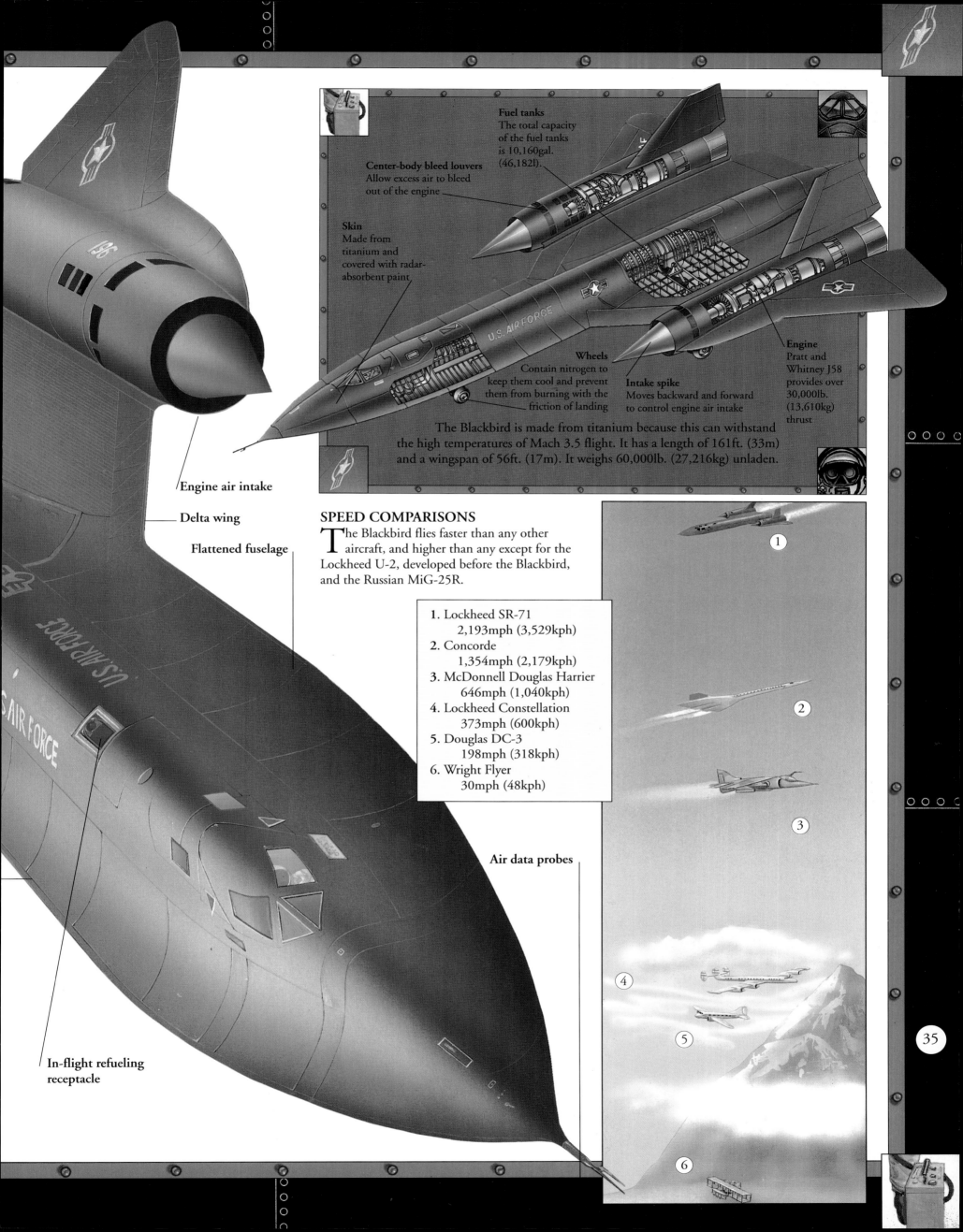

Fuel tanks
The total capacity of the fuel tanks is 10,160gal. (46,182l).

Center-body bleed louvers
Allow excess air to bleed out of the engine

Skin
Made from titanium and covered with radar-absorbent paint

Wheels
Contain nitrogen to keep them cool and prevent them from burning with the friction of landing

Intake spike
Moves backward and forward to control engine air intake

Engine
Pratt and Whitney J58 provides over 30,000lb. (13,610kg) thrust

The Blackbird is made from titanium because this can withstand the high temperatures of Mach 3.5 flight. It has a length of 161ft. (33m) and a wingspan of 56ft. (17m). It weighs 60,000lb. (27,216kg) unladen.

Engine air intake

Delta wing

Flattened fuselage

U.S. AIR FORCE

Air data probes

In-flight refueling receptacle

SPEED COMPARISONS

The Blackbird flies faster than any other aircraft, and higher than any except for the Lockheed U-2, developed before the Blackbird, and the Russian MiG-25R.

1. Lockheed SR-71
   2,193mph (3,529kph)
2. Concorde
   1,354mph (2,179kph)
3. McDonnell Douglas Harrier
   646mph (1,040kph)
4. Lockheed Constellation
   373mph (600kph)
5. Douglas DC-3
   198mph (318kph)
6. Wright Flyer
   30mph (48kph)

Hoverfly

*"What's surprising . . . for an aircraft with
such extraordinary flying characteristics . . .
is it's very easy to fly."*
Captain Charles "Chuck" Maloney,
American Harrier pilot

This unusual military aircraft was developed during
the 1960s and first flew in 1967. The Harrier is
capable of flying in ways that are impossible for other
aircraft. It can take off and land vertically like a
helicopter, which has earned it the name "Jump Jet."
This means that it can be used during warfare even if
runways are destroyed. It can also hover motionless in
the sky and even fly backward! A single lever controls
the position of the plane's engine nozzles, which gives
this aircraft its special mobility. The nozzles are rotated
to point downward or backward by moving the lever.
Sitting on an ejector seat, the pilot commands this fast-
attack aircraft from a cockpit with good all-around
visibility. The Harrier can carry a selection of missiles
and bombs. Two gun pods under the fuselage
can each hold 100 shells.

FLYING GEAR

Harrier pilots wear
a pressure suit
with a life preserver,
which inflates if they
ditch in the sea. The
suit also squeezes the
pilot's legs
when the
Harrier makes
sharp turns.
This stops
blood from
draining from
the pilot's head.

VERTICAL TAKEOFF

The arrows on the diagram above show the
direction the plane is flying. Before the plane
takes off, the engine nozzles point downward.
The pilot opens the throttle near his left thigh to
increase the engine's thrust, and the plane rises
vertically. The pilot then rotates the engine
nozzles until they point backward, and the blast
of exhaust gases pushes the plane forward.

Cooling air intake

Rocket pod

Tail radar

Air brake

SKI JUMP

The Harrier can carry more fuel and
weapons if it takes off from a
runway instead of vertically. This is
because vertical takeoff uses more power. The Harrier's takeoff run can
be shortened by sloping the end of the runway upward. This is especially
useful when Harriers operate from aircraft carriers. These ships have a
sloped deck called a "ski jump." A Harrier with a heavy load can take to
the air from this runway. On its return, and with a lighter load, the
Harrier can land vertically. This is the safest way to land on a ship's deck.

ENGINE

The blast of exhaust gas is directed from the engine through four nozzles that can be rotated. This provides the thrust to power the Harrier.

Canopy
Gives pilot 360° visibility

Engine
About 21,516lb. (9,760kg) thrust

Fuel tank
Located behind the engine

Engine nozzle
There are four of these geared together so they all point in the same direction.

Outrigger wheel
Helps to steady aircraft

Wing-tip jet
Controls the plane's position when it hovers

Rack
Racks under each wing carry bombs, missiles and fuel tanks.

The Harrier AV8-A has a maximum speed of 646mph (1,040kph) and a length of 46ft. (14.12m).

Auxiliary air intake

In-flight refueling probe

Yaw vane

Cockpit air intake

Gun pod

CONTROL LEVERS

The nozzle lever controls the angle of the engine exhaust nozzles. The throttle increases the engine's thrust. The Short Takeoff Stop and Vertical Takeoff Stop mark the places for the nozzle lever to be positioned to take off from ski jumps (short takeoff), or to take off vertically.

1. Throttle
2. Short Takeoff Stop
3. Nozzle lever
4. Vertical Takeoff Stop

INSTRUMENT PANEL

Screens display radar warning, navigation and engine data, as well as the weapons status and a map that shows the land beneath the Harrier as it is flying. The most important data, such as speed, altitude and any possible threat, is projected on a glass plate, or "head-up display," in the pilot's line of sight.

37

Faster than sound

"It's the closest thing to space travel I'm ever likely to experience, yet it seemed so normal. Concorde really is a remarkable aircraft. It gives you the opportunity to be a shirt-sleeve astronaut."
Peter Johnson, a Concorde passenger

Concorde is the world's first supersonic commercial passenger aircraft operating regular scheduled flights. Concorde was developed jointly by Britain and France during the 1960s and 1970s, when the DC-3, the Constellation and the Comet 4s were in regular service. No other aircraft can match Concorde's dreamlike performance and comfort. Nor can any other aircraft fly faster than sound over great distances without requiring in-flight refueling. A few military aircraft can fly faster, but they need in-flight refueling to fly as far. Concorde flies high through the atmosphere on the edge of space. At an altitude of 12mi. (18km), flying at 1,354mph (2,179kph), passengers can see the curve of the earth's surface. But there is no sensation of speed. The aircraft seems to hang motionless in the air, yet the lightning speed makes the windows feel warm because of friction with the air outside.

PASSENGER SERVICE

The above map shows how Concorde has improved flight times across the world. This ability to fly so quickly and in such style has made Concorde an important service for the business community.

1. Transatlantic route: 2 hr. 54.5 min. by Concorde, 65 hr. by *Hindenburg* airship
2. South African route: 8 hr. 8 min. by Concorde, 24 hr. by de Havilland Comet
3. Australian route: 17 hr. 13min. by Concorde, 55 hr. 7 min. by Lockheed Constellation

DROOP-SNOOT

Concorde's nose was designed to "droop," to give a clear view ahead for takeoff and landing (1). The nose is raised for normal flight (2).

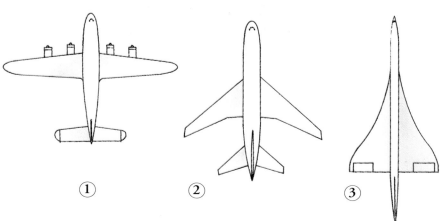

WING POSITIONS

The faster a plane is designed to fly, the more its wings have to be swept back. A piston-engined plane has straight wings (1). A jet airliner's wings are angled at 25-40 degrees (2). Concorde's wings are swept back so much that they form a triangular "delta" shape (3).